by Deborah Melissa Möller

© Copyright 2011 – Deborah Melissa Möller

ISBN-13: 978-1480215900

ISBN-10: 1480215902

License Notes

Thank you for purchasing this book. You are welcome to share it with your friends. This book may be reproduced, copied and distributed for non-commercial purposes, provided the book remains in its complete original form. If you enjoyed this book, please return to Amazon.com or Smashwords.com to discover other works by this author. Thank you for your support.

All Scripture reference and notes are from the Recovery Version Bible.

Text editors: Adri Malan & Ellie Landman

www.CreateHisImage.co.za

AUTHOR'S ACKNOWLEDGEMENTS

I want to thank God the Father, Jesus Christ His Son and His Holy Spirit for entrusting me with this task to do the will of the Father. Thank You for calling me before the foundation of the world to help call forth Your precious Bride. Thank you for Your grace and mercy. Thank you for being my God, for being my Father, for being my King, for being my Helper for You inspire and bless me daily. I love You, my Lord!

I want to thank those who pray for me daily and always loving me and accepting me for being me. I especially want to thank my family and friends.

I want to thank Adri Malan and Ellie Landman for their help in editing this book.

Glory to the Father!

Glory to the Son!

Glory to the Spirit!

These Three are One!

TABLE OF CONTENTS

INTRODUCTION	5
Chapter 1: COME OUT OF EGYPT	8
Chapter 2: LET MY PEOPLE GO!	12
Chapter 3: THE PROMISED LAND	16
Chapter 4: MY MANNA	19
Chapter 5: RIVERS IN THE DESERT	24
Chapter 6: THE SEED IN GOOD SOIL	28
Chapter 7: MY PRECIOUS BRIDE	33
Chapter 8: THE WEDDING FEAST IS READY	37
Chapter 9: MY COMMANDMENTS	41
Chapter 10: MY TORCHBEARERS	47
PRAYER	50

INTRODUCTION

While reading in **Matt. 3:3 "For this is he who was spoken of through Isaiah the prophet, saying, "A voice of one crying in the wilderness, Prepare the way of the Lord; make straight His paths."**, the Lord started speaking to me.

The Lord said: "This is it, My child. You stand on the brink of your creation purpose. This I created you for. Keep in step with Me, I shall refine you, for the task you are about to do requires great responsibility. Like My servant Moses".

I then said to the Lord that I have so many faults and weaknesses and sin – and that He just cannot use me for this.

The Lord replied: "I choose you. I created you for this purpose, which is about to swing open like double doors. You will be My representative. I will anoint you as My end-time Moses. Many you will lead out of Egypt. The seeking ones will listen.

This will be the introduction for the second book you are about to write. You will be My voice for many cannot hear Me because of idols and hardened hearts and many do not make time for Me. As in the days of old, I will again rise up My prophets and they will speak with authority given by the Father.

Many things are about to happen on earth. Truly, we are at the beginning of the end. My John the Baptists will cry out of the wilderness: **"...Prepare the way of the Lord; make straight His paths."**

My child, just obey and love Me as you do. I will lead you and speak to you. Do exactly as I instruct you. Religion will came against you, but learn from Me. Religion also came against Me. The more I told the truth, the more religion questioned Me, the more they persecuted Me. Therefore count yourself blessed, that you are persecuted for My Name's sake."

"Blessed are those who are persecuted for the sake of righteousness, for theirs is the kingdom of the heavens. Rejoice and exult, for your reward is great in the heavens; for so they persecuted the prophets who were before you." (Matt. 5:10,12)

"Run with the horses My child!"

"If you have run with footmen and they have wearied you, how then will you compete with horses?..." (Jer. 12:5)

"I will direct your path into righteousness. I will direct you to Me and straight into the Father's bosom. The Father and I are one".

THE JOURNEY

On 20 July 2010, the Lord said the following to me:

"You are going to write a book about the end-time. It is your creation purpose." I then sensed the Lord saying that it was not going to be easy, because people would not take it, except for the remnant. The book will be for the remnant, for His Bride. The book will be about the preparation for the King's return and for those who did not know, to be warned.

"This will be a gift for My Bride. It is for those who love Me, for those who are seeking the Truth, who called out 'Lord, tell us more, only the truth Lord'. The book will be about Jesus. Jesus is the key, Jesus must be your focus and Jesus is your destiny."

All this is recorded in the first book, *The Final Call*, which started on 22 April 2011 when the Lord instructed me to write down all He says. The book you are holding in your hand, *The Exodus*, is the second book. The Lord revealed at the end of this second book, that He is preparing me to write down the third book.

I am only obedient in doing the will of the Father. In 2009, I started praying that the Lord will show me the absolute truth about Him and the end-time. He is indeed revealing the truth to me. And, as I freely received, I should freely give.

Chapter 1

COME OUT OF EGYPT

1 July 2011

"My people are trapped in chains, like iron hands. They cannot move forward because of these chains. They cannot see for these chains are binding them in the spiritual realm. This has a direct influence in the natural realm. For whatever you bind on earth will be bound in heaven. Like a chain gate that stands before them and Me. While you feed it, it will grow. For what you eat and see, you will become. This eating is eating Me or eating the world.

My people, how I long for you to be released from this self-made prison that you build around yourself. Your own little iron castle. You think you are protected within the walls you put around yourself – the world you build around yourself daily. Where is your focus? On Me or on the world? You cannot serve two masters, for you will love the one and hate the other.

My people, you are ensnared by the world and the prince of this world (Pharaoh). You are in bondage and in this bondage you are slaves to Pharaoh. Not only are you under judgment under Pharaoh, but because of your sin and disobedience you are also under judgment from Me. In this you suffer, My children.

Will you call on Me with a clean heart and hands and ask that I deliver you out of the house of bondage that you find yourself in? If you call on Me in humbleness, I will hear you and I will deliver you and save you. Many of My people are so much part of the world (Egypt) that they do not even discern that they are of the world. Yet I said "**...do not be fashioned according to this age, but be**

transformed by the renewing of the mind..." (Rom. 12:2)
The flesh profits nothing. The Spirit brings life.

Those of My children who have become part of the world, and do not yet realise this, will start to realise this enslavement - this real bondage for the floods of slavery has now been opened. More will be "*needed*" by the prince of this world. The Pharaoh demands that you compromise much more. If you are weak, you will be pushed into greater compromise and you will be enslaved with chains of heavier iron. The more you are in this world, the less you will know about Me or even hear Me when I call you."

I WILL RAISE UP MY PROPHETS

"Many are entrapped in this iron castle of worldliness. Because of this, I will raise up My prophets, My Moses' to speak on My behalf, to be My representatives. I will anoint them to lead My people out of Egypt. For the enslavement is about to become so severe that you will call for Me to come forth and set you free.

For many it will be a slow and difficult process to get out of the worldly lifestyle because they are stiff-necked and have hardened their hearts. For they have eaten Egyptian food for many years and they are used to the luxuries and pleasures that the world has given them. Are you willing to lose your soul-life, in order to gain a fruitful life?

If you are obedient and follow as I lead you out of the worldly, fleshly and Egyptian lifestyle, your fruit and sprouts will spring up quickly and with burden and pain you will walk the path that will lead to righteousness. If you listen and obey, you will hear Me when I say not to turn to your right nor to your left, but to keep on this road. Are you willing?"

"And everyone who has left houses or brothers or sisters or father or mother or children or fields for My name's sake shall receive a hundred times as much and shall inherit eternal life." (Matt. 19:29)

ENSLAVEMENT IN EGYPT

"I know the end from the beginning. Just as in the days of My servant Moses, so shall it be again in the end-time. My people will be enslaved in the world. The enslavement will be reinforced. Conditions and rules will be hard and unfair. Will My people come out of the world (Egypt) into the desert to walk with Me? Are you ready to leave the meat and milk of Egypt and follow Me? I will burn everything with fire when I come to test all things. Only that which was done for My Name in the will of the Father will remain. Do not be naive. All your works and words will be judged.

My children, you are currently in that place where you murmured. You murmured against and over the land, over each other. You have no control over these things. You are enslaved in Egypt. You are enslaved by the prince of the world, Pharaoh. And he is putting new burdens on you each day. While you are in the world, you will eat what is given to you. I allow it, because the more unrighteousness and unfairness happens in the land, the more you will realise that you need Me, your God. For I am the God of Abraham, God of Isaac, God of Jacob. You need to ask Me to deliver you from the net of the fowler. Ask Me to deliver you out of the bondage of slavery. For if you remain, you will surely die with the plagues that I will be pouring out over Egypt, the worldly land, poisoned by greed of man, lust of man, rebellion and sin.

Choose My camp or Pharaoh's camp, for the plaques will surely touch you in Pharaoh's camp. In My camp, I will protect you and no plague will come near your tent. Choose today - life or death, blessing or curse!"

Chapter 2

LET MY PEOPLE GO!

2 July 2011

"I will be like a fire to you at night. I will be like a cloud to you at day. My presence will be with you day and night, if you come out of the world, out of Egypt. You cannot worship Me in Egypt, for the fumes of Egypt and all the pleasures leave a bad odour and taste. You will not see My glory while you are in Egypt (worldly living).

I am going to make a way for you to escape out of Egypt so that you can worship Me in the desert. In the desert I will test you and refine you and then will follow the Promised Land. My Son, Jesus, will bring you into the Promised Land.

Therefore, surrender your soul-life, the life that you fill with soulish things. There are 24 hours in a day. How do you spend it? Do you make more time to relax than to spend time in My company? This is your test if you are in Egypt – the time you spend with Me vs. soulish interest. You be the judge on your own life and time".

REMOVING THE LUKEWARM

"You will find that your lives in Egypt will become even dryer and dryer and you will thirst more and more. Because I am removing the lukewarm, you will only be hot or cold. Either you are for me, or against Me. No more sitting on the fence, playing church and playing religious games. You choose either light or darkness. I am going to remove the pretence; the masks will fall off the people's faces. People will understand and see if you are for Me or against Me. Either hot or cold. For if you do not come out of Egypt, you will grow cold. I will lead My people out of Egypt and I will dwell among them in the desert. If you remain in Egypt, you will be killed by the plagues."

RELIGION AND TRADITIONS

"As in the days of My servant, Moses and My people Israel, there will again be a great exodus. All this will happen in the Spirit. Many with eyes open will see this move and will partake of it. With this move, many will be mocked and persecuted for many people cling to religion and traditions. Religion and traditions kill the working of My Spirit and the work of My true servants. Those that oppose My truth will be judged and you will not prevail against My true prophets, for I made them a pillar of bronze."

"And I am now making you today into a fortified city and into an iron pillar and into bronze walls against the whole land, against the kings of Judah, against its princes, against its priests, and against the people of the land. And they will fight against you, but they will not prevail against you; for I am with you, declares Jehovah, to deliver you." (Jer. 1:18-19)

"Religion, tradition, Satan and the world... let My people go, so that they can dwell with Me and worship Me in the desert. For I can make water run in the desert. I can make bitter water sweet. With man it is impossible, but with God all is possible. Let My people go, so that they can come in Oneness, so that they can be One Body, One Bride, for if My Body unites, without division, Satan trembles.

Let My people go! For you are slaves under a demonic system. If you come to Me, you will be My servants and I will bless you and your fruit will multiply. You need to become like children, for children are free. In Egypt, you will not roam free. You will remain in bondage. Follow Me, listen to Me, and obey Me. **This will be the last exodus**, for everything that happened in the beginning will again happen in the end. The plagues have already begun. Can you discern it in your country? Do you discern the plagues that are happening in the Spirit? Water will turn into blood, frogs, lice, flies, pestilence, boils, hail, locusts, darkness, death of the first born. All these plagues will be unleashed on the people and the land to let My people go! You will then realise that it is time to follow Me out of Egypt into the desert. With this, you will focus on Me, for I should be your focus and daily living, not worldly pleasures."

YOUR LEADER

"Your generation is again looking for a leader – some great leader to stand up and take control. Still you want a Saul. Why can't you understand that I must be your leader? Man can lead you away from Me. Why don't you call on Me and I will lead you daily and you will have My protection if you call on Me. You just murmur to one another and still more evil and frogs come out of your mouths. Evil fire is spewed over the people, yet you cannot do anything because you are not dealing with human power, but with evil demonic power. Only by My power will I quench the Pharaoh. Only I can open the red sea (the way) and kill all those who oppose you, enslave and bind you. How long will I wait until you call on Me to lead you out of Egypt and to be your only leader?

Turn your focus to Me, the Lord. Remove your focus from people for they will not be able to help you. If you cling to people, a system or religion, you will stay behind. Only if I am your ALL in all, your everything, your Creator, your first Love, I will lead you out and I will lead you by My fire and My cloud.

Come take this step of faith with Me. Leave the security of Egypt and walk with Me as I lead you into My freedom. For only I can give you freedom. No man can ever give you freedom. It is I that set free!"

Chapter 3

THE PROMISED LAND

3 July 2011

"As the ripe barley determines the beginning of the New Year, so I will show when the exodus will occur. You will know by My Spirit. You better be prepared so that you do not miss My exodus. For I will make the way for you and you will follow Me. Even if things look impossible, I will make the way. I will, by My power, show you that I am your Redeemer and Saviour. I will set you free.

I will make a covenant with you that, if you obey Me and love Me, I will lead you into the Promised Land. Your focus should remain on Me, for if you look at your circumstances, you will recall to mind your Egyptian lifestyle. Many are lost in Egypt (the world)."

JESUS IS THE TRUTH

"When I sent My Son to represent Me on earth, many followed Him because of the miracles and the wonders He did. Many followed Him to get touched by Him, to get healed. But not many remained with Him to the end, though He continually spoke the truth. He only spoke what He heard from Me. Learn from His life. Don't just follow My Son to get healed or touched. Follow Him because you love Him and you want to abide in the truth. If you take your eyes from the truth and focus on yourself (your flesh), you will stumble and fall. If you follow My Son for the truth, He will lead you to Me, your Father, Who is your destination.

Through My Son and the Spirit you will touch Me. Seek Me and you will find the truth. We want to dwell with man, to fill man, to be part of Us. We, the Son, the Spirit, and the Father dwell with each other. We are divinely One, yet Three. So We want to impart and dwell with man, divinely one, yet God and man, for we want man to become like Us in life and nature, but not in the Godhead."

RESTORING THE LAND OF MILK AND HONEY

"We are looking for people who are willing to settle in Our wilderness temporarily. This is so that We can refine you, build you and make you ready for the Millennium (Promised land). Restoring the earth in the Millennium will be the restoration of the land of milk and honey. My people, if I send Our spies to have a lookout in the Promised land, thereby, bringing word from Me about the Millennium, know that I do not lie. It will indeed be a land flowing of milk and honey. There will be great riches and fruit. Do not lose your faith and murmur, for I will send you the truth about My land. Know that I know what is best for you and that My plans are to do you good, not evil. Don't lose your faith in the wilderness. Don't look back at Egypt. Remember what happened to Lot's wife when she looked back one more time?"

"**...He said, Escape for your life. Do not look behind you, neither stay anywhere in the plain..." (Gen 19:17)**

"**But his wife looked back from behind him, and she became a pillar of salt." (Gen. 19:26)**

"**Remember Lot's wife. Whoever seeks to preserve his soul-life will lose it, and whoever loses it will preserve it alive". (Luke 17:32-33)**

"My people, you need to know if I send you out in the midst of your slave master and I point you the way, it will be the point of no return. If you lose your faith, you will die in the wilderness."

"But he who has endured to the end, this one shall be saved". (Matt. 24:13)

"When you focus on Me and not your circumstances, you will keep your faith and I, the Lord Jesus, will take you into the Promised land. I will be like a Joshua leading you over the river Jordan."

Chapter 4

MY MANNA

4 July 2011

"Just as My son ascended into heaven, likewise He will come again on the clouds. Everything will come full circle. Everything that happened in the beginning will happen at the end. Just like the two trees in Genesis (the beginning) and the two trees in Revelation (the end). It is a matter of eating and drinking in Genesis (the beginning), as it is a matter of eating and drinking in Revelation (the end). What has begun, will be completed. It will come full circle!

My people, as you find yourself out of Egypt and in the wilderness, I will feed you. I will give you My manna. My manna is My daily word, which I will feed you. This will be enough to sustain you daily. It will bring you enough nourishment. It is very important that you eat this manna, which I will give to you daily. It will build you up, for you are to receive the sword, the two-edged sword that is needed in your mouth. Do not long for the meat, the Egyptian food that you left behind. You should keep your focus on Me.

I will also provide you with a river of water from Me. Drink from My life-giving fountain. If you drink this, you will by no means thirst. Your focus in the wilderness will be to eat and drink Me! Eating and drinking was important in the beginning (Genesis). Eating and drinking is important in the end. The matter of eating and drinking is very important. It is a basic principle!"

"And out of the ground Jehovah God caused to grow every tree that is pleasant to the sight and good for food, as well

as the tree of life in the middle of the garden and the tree of the knowledge of good and evil." (Gen. 2:9)

"And on this side and on that side of the river was the tree of life, producing twelve fruits, yielding its fruit each month; and the leaves of the tree are for the healing of the nations." (Rev. 22:2)

"And a river went forth from Eden to water the garden, and from there it divided and became four branches". (Gen. 2:10)

"And he showed me a river of water of life, bright as crystal, proceeding out of the throne of God and of the Lamb in the middle of its street." (Rev. 22:1)

FREELY GIVE AS YOU FREELY RECEIVED

"If you seek in your heart to hear Me, if you seek to hear My voice, if you desire that I speak to you as a friend, then ask that from Me. I will search your heart for I know your deepest parts. If you ask Me with a clean heart and hands and you obey Me, I will speak to you. But take note: As I freely give to you, you must freely give to others. If I make known to you a revelation or a secret and I instruct you to reveal it to others, you must do so."

"And his master answered and said to him, Evil and slothful slave, you knew that I reap where I did not sow and gather where I did not winnow. Therefore you should have deposited my money with the money changers; and when I came, I would have recovered what is mine with interest. Take away therefore the talent from him and give **it to him who has the ten talents. For to everyone who has, more shall be given, and he shall abound; but from him who does not have, even that which he has shall be** taken away from him. And cast out the useless slave into the outer darkness. In that place there will be the weeping and the gnashing of teeth." (Matt. 25:26-30)

"And the disciples came and said to Him, Why do You speak in parables to them? And He answered and said to them, Because to you it has been given to know the mysteries of the kingdom of the heavens, but to them it has not been given. For whoever has, it shall be given to him, and he will abound; but whoever does not have, even that which he has shall be taken away from him. For this reason I speak to them in parables, because seeing they do not see, and hearing they do not hear, nor do they understand." (Matt. 13:10-13)

"Therefore be wise in your asking from Me. If you have a desire to know Me better, to be very close to Me, I will draw you near to Me. It is still your free-will choice how close I can come to you. When you surrender, I can be the Potter and you the clay and I will mould you into the image of My Son. For I want many sons!"

"And we know that all things work together for good to those who love God, to those who are called according to His purpose. Because those whom He foreknew, He also predestined to be conformed to the image of His Son, that He might be the Firstborn among many brothers; And those whom He predestined, these He also called; and those whom He called, these He also justified; and those whom He justified, these He also glorified." (Rom. 8:28-29)

FIGHT YOUR FLESH

"How similar is your daily lives to Israel, My people in the wilderness? You always find something to murmur about. Why is this? Am I not your all-sufficient supplier? When you live by the Spirit and not by the flesh, you will have nothing to murmur or worry about. For your eyes will be steadfast on Me and your eating and drinking will be Me. Your flesh is your greatest enemy. You need to fight your flesh. If you become thirsty and you cannot perceive Me, know that you dwell in the flesh. This you must know, you are in the flesh when you thirst and murmur. Call on My Name, for if you call on Me, I will fight with you and fill you with My Spirit and you will start drinking from My life-giving Spirit. This is a daily and moment-by-moment choice you need to make. Choose to walk in the Spirit. The flesh will profit nothing. Through the flesh it will be a difficult journey and the works will be in vain. Walk in the Spirit by calling on Me, eating and drinking Me and waiting on Me. Then I will fill you with oil and you will be full of the revelation of who I AM"

"That the God of our Lord Jesus Christ, the Father of glory, may give to you a spirit of wisdom and revelation in the full knowledge of Him, the eyes of your heart having been enlightened, that you may know what is the hope of His calling, and what are the riches of the glory of His inheritance in the saints..." (Eph. 1:17-18)

"Ask this, that I give you the wisdom and revelation of who I am.

O My people, My Word I speak over and over to you. The desires of My heart I tell you over and over. I never change. I am always the same. I desire for you to love Me with you whole heart, and mind, and soul, and to love your neighbour as yourself. I speak My Word over and over. Who will listen and obey? Time is running out. I have spoken. I spoke through My prophets, spoke through people not even knowing Me. I sent warnings, continually. As you will be aware by now, many things are busy shaking. I am shaking life, nature and you. You will see it with your eyes. Do watch out for Me, otherwise I will come as a thief."

"Blessed are those slaves whom the master, when he comes, will find watching. Truly I tell you that he will gird himself and will have them recline at table, and he will come to them and serve them. And if he comes in the second watch, or if in the third, and finds them so, blessed are those slaves. But know this, that if the master of the house had known in what hour the thief was coming, he would not have allowed his house to be broken into. You also, be ready, because at an hour when you do not expect it, the Son of Man is coming." (Luke 12:37-40)

"My people, if you overcome the flesh, you overcome the world (Egypt)."

"Take My yoke upon you and learn from Me, for I am meek and lowly in heart, and you will find rest for your souls. For My yoke is easy and My burden is light." (Matt. 11:29-30)

"If you want to follow Me, you need to take up your cross daily. Learn from My life!"

Chapter 5

RIVERS IN THE DESERT

5 July 2011

"But now thus says Jehovah who created you, O Jacob, and who formed you, O Israel: Do not fear, because I have redeemed you; I have called you by your name; you are Mine. When pass through the waters, I will be with you, and through the rivers, they will not flow over you. And when you walk through the fire, you will not be burned, and the flame will not consume you.

Because I am Jehovah your God, the Holy One of Israel, your Saviour, I have given Egypt as your ransom, Cush and Seba instead of you. Since you were precious in My eyes, since you have been honourable and I have loved you, I will give up men in your place, and people in exchange for your life.

Do not fear, because I am with you; I will bring your seed from the east and gather you from the west. I will say to the north, Give them up, and to the south, do not keep them back. Bring My sons from afar, and My daughters from the end of the earth, everyone who is called by My name, whom I have created, formed, and even made for My glory.

Bring out the people who are blind yet have eyes, and those who are deaf yet have ears. Let all the nations be gathered together, and let the people assemble. Who among them can declare this and relate to us the former things? Let them bring forth their witnesses, that they may be justified, and let them hear and say, It is true.

You are My witnesses, declares Jehovah, and My servant whom I have chosen, in order that you may know and believe Me and understand that I am He. Before Me there was no God formed, neither will there be any after Me.

I, even I, am Jehovah; and there is no Saviour besides Me.

I have declared, and I have saved, and I have let them hear; There is no strange god among you. And you are My witnesses, declares Jehovah, and I am God.

Indeed, before the day was, I am He, and there is no one who can deliver from My hand. I will work and who will reverse it?

Thus says Jehovah, your Redeemer, the Holy One of Israel, for your sake I have sent to Babylon, and I will bring down all of them as fugitives, even the Chaldeans, whose rejoicing is in the ships.

I am Jehovah, your Holy One, the Creator of Israel, your King.

Thus says Jehovah, Who has made a way in the sea, and a path in the mighty waters, Who brings forth the chariot and the horse, the army and the powerful together. They will lie down, they will not rise; They are extinct, they are quenched like flax.

Do not call to mind the former things, nor consider the things of old. Indeed, I am doing a new thing; It will now spring forth; Do you not know it? I will even make a way in the wilderness, rivers in the desert.

The animals of the field will honour Me, the jackals and the ostriches, because I have given them water in the wilderness, rivers in the desert, to give a drink to My people, My chosen ones. This people I have formed for Myself; They will show forth My praise.

But you have not called upon Me, O Jacob, but you have grown weary of Me, O Israel. You have not brought Me a sheep for your burnt offerings, and you have not honoured Me with your sacrifices; I have not made you serve Me with meal offering, nor wearied you with incense. You did not buy calamus for Me with money, and you did not fill Me with the fat of your sacrifices. Indeed, you have burdened Me with your sins; you have wearied Me with your iniquities.

I, even I, am He who wipes away your transgressions for My own sake, and I will not remember your sins. Put Me in remembrance; let us plead in judgement together: Declare your case that you may be justified. Your first father sinned, and your mediators transgressed against Me.

Therefore I profaned the princes of the sanctuary, and I delivered up Jacob to destruction and Israel to reviling." (Isa. 43)

"For My words are true and righteous. Who is there that can compete with Me? There is no other God than Me. I created the heavens and the earth and all the stars. I name each one. My precious children, be encouraged, I am for you. Who can be against you?

I will carry you in time of difficulty. I will look after you. I will never leave you or forsake you. For I am the rivers running in the wilderness. I will refresh you. I will give you rest. Lean on Me, trust Me, and surrender to Me!"

Chapter 6

THE SEED IN GOOD SOIL

6 July 2011

"Listen! Behold, the sower went out to sow.

And as he sowed, some seed fell beside the way, and the birds came and devoured it.

And other seed fell on the rocky place, where it did not have much earth, and immediately it sprang up because it had no depth of earth. And when the sun rose, it was scorched; and because it had no root, it withered.

And other seed fell into the thorns, and the thorns came up and utterly choked it, and it yielded no fruit.

And others fell into the good earth and yielded fruit, coming up and growing; and one bore thirty-fold, and one sixty-fold, and one a hundred-fold.

And He said, He who has ears to hear, let him hear. And when He was alone, those around Him, with the twelve, asked Him about the parables. And He said to them, To you it has been given to know the mystery of the kingdom of God, but to those outside, all things are in parables, In order that seeing they may see and not perceive, and hearing they may hear and not understand, lest they turn and it be forgiven them.   And He said to them, do you not know this parable? And how will you know all the parables?

The sower sows the word.

And these are the ones beside the way, where the word is sown; and when they hear, immediately Satan comes and takes away the word which has been sown into them.

And likewise, these are the ones being sown on the rocky places, who, when they hear the word, immediately receive it with joy. Yet they have no root in themselves, but last only for a time; then when affliction or persecution occurs because of the word, immediately they are stumbled.

And others are the ones being sown into the thorns; these are the ones who have heard the word, and the anxieties of the age and the deceitfulness of riches and the lusts for other things enter in and utterly choke the word, and it becomes unfruitful.

And these are the ones sown on the good earth: those who hear the word and receive it and bear fruit, one thirtyfold, and one sixtyfold, and one a hundredfold." (Mark 4:3-20)

"My people, be watchful that you hear the word and receive it and bear fruit. Therefore, My people, you need to walk with Me through trials and tribulations so that you will be able to discern Me as the Truth; so that you will be able to stand when affliction or persecution come; so that you can come out of the world and not get trapped in deceitfulness of riches and the lust for other things.

Come back to your first love. Love Me for I first loved you. Come into relationship with Me, for I want to give you of My daily bread and wine. Come eat and drink Me, for the more you eat and drink

Me, the more you will speak like Me. For if you abide in Me, as I abide in the Father, We will be one.

My people perish because of a lack of knowledge. But if you seek Me, you will find the Truth. Many seek for the truth and get entrapped by divers things that they perceive as the truth. But if you seek Me, you will find the Truth, for it is written, first seek the kingdom of God and all things will be added unto you."

COME INTO RELATIONSHIP

"The longer you walk with Us, the deeper the relationship grows. The more you grow, the more you will realise that if you gain Christ, you have gained everything. For the Father and the Son is one. Because of Christ, you gain the Father. We desire for you to have a relationship with Us. O, My people, this is of such importance, for if you have Us and are one with Us, you won't need anything. You will be in the perfect plan of God's economy (God's plan). You will walk in your ordained purpose, predestined before the foundation of the world.

Come close My child. Only I can protect you, lead you, help you, save you. I am closer than a brother. I love you much more than your mother and I will count you a friend!

Call on Me, call My Name. Seek Me. Inquire of Me. Call Me in truthfulness. Will you love Me above all else? Am I your first love? Will you follow Me and obey Me when I speak to you? If I ask "whom shall I send" will you answer? Or will you run away? I tell you: **"Whoever seeks to preserve his soul-life will lose it, and whoever loses it will preserve it alive." (Luke 17:33)**

"I am the light in the darkness. If you stand with Me, the darkness cannot come near you. Great darkness is busy spreading on the earth. If you are not in the light, you will be in the darkness. In the darkness you will die. Watch therefore that your focus remains on Me and as I move, you need to move with Me. Even in the wilderness I need to fight with you, for you to stand your ground. Keep in step with Me, in this wilderness, day by day, moment by moment. I will lead you up My mountain. On the mountain, you will see My face.

My people, if you come before Me, you need to sanctify yourself. Because I've sanctified Myself, you can do so also".

"And for their sake I sanctify Myself, that they themselves also may be sanctified in truth." (John 17:19)

"My child, if you lack faith, ask and it shall be given to you. For because of your faith, you can be healed, set free and restored. For you need faith to finish this race. If you set your eyes on Me, your faith would be strengthened. Do not be of this world. Ask that you will be protected from the evil one."

"I do not ask that You would take them out of the world, but that You would keep them out of **the hands of the evil one." (John 17:15)**

"I know that you have many needs and wants ... **for your Father knows the things that you have need of before you ask Him. You then pray in this way: Our Father who is in the heavens, Your name be sanctified; Your kingdom come; Your will be done, as in heaven, so also on earth. Give us today our daily bread. And forgive us our debts, as we also have forgiven our debtors. And do not bring us into temptation, but deliver us from the evil one. For Yours is the kingdom and the power and the glory forever. Amen." (Matt. 6:8-13)**

"The ultimate heart's desire that We have for Our people is: **"…that they may know You, the only true God, and Him whom You have sent, Jesus Christ." (John 17:3)** And this is eternal life!"

Chapter 7

MY PRECIOUS BRIDE

7 July 2011

"You are My precious possession. For I love you and I long for you to come under My shadow, in My secret place. My mercies are new every morning. Come closer, for I am patiently awaiting you. Come closer so that you can see the fullness of My plan."

"And Moses went up to God, and Jehovah called to him out of the mountain, saying, Thus you shall say to the house of Jacob and tell the children of Israel: You have seen what I did to the Egyptians and how I bore you on eagles' wings and brought you to Myself. Now therefore if you will indeed obey My voice and keep My covenant, then you shall be My personal treasure from among all peoples, for all the earth is Mine. And you shall be to Me a kingdom of priests and a holy nation..." (Exo. 19:3-6).

"My Spirit will bear you up and out of Egypt like My eagles' wings and bring you to Me, if you ask that from Me. Just as I brought them (the Israelites), out of Egypt so I will again bring My people out of Satan's persecution during the great tribulation."

"And the woman fled into the wilderness, where she has a place there prepared by God so that they might nourish her there a thousand two hundred and sixty days." (Rev. 12:6).

"And to the woman there were given the two wings of the great eagle that she might fly into the wilderness into her

place, where she is nourished for a time and times and half a time from the face of the serpent." (Rev. 12:14)

"For I will indeed nourish you in the wilderness. For a time you will be fed, and I will take My Bride."

"And she brought forth a son, a man-child, who is to shepherd all the nations with an iron rod; and her child was caught up to God and to His throne." (Rev. 12:5)

A GIFT FROM THE FATHER

"My precious Bride, I will come and rapture you, for you loved Me, obeyed Me, and you overcame the system of this world. Because you loved Me and honoured Me first in your life, I will lift you up before the Father, for you will be My precious Bride. I so adore you! You ravish My heart, My Bride! The wedding feast will be your gift to Me from the Father. We will then come in full oneness and unity, for you and Me, the Bride and Bridegroom will make an everlasting covenant that will stand for all eternity.

This wedding day was divinely appointed and prepared before the foundation of the world. For on this day, God will be fully in man and man in God (not in the Godhead). We will be divinely mingled and you will have authority to rule nations with an iron rod. O My Bride, many things await you, for you cannot fathom what will be revealed to you. My Father will surprise you and you will be blessed and you will be called blessed of the Lord. For you will be the Wife of the Lamb and we will be one, as I and the Father are One. You were made in Our image to fulfil this very purpose: Us and you becoming one. This will be the New Jerusalem! This will be a grand and awesome and marvellous event. It will be talked about forever! For you will receive the mark of the Bride, the wife of the Lamb and you will have this mark forever! What a privilege! For you are My precious treasure and you are Mine!

Yet, My people, many of My Body (My Church) will stay behind in the wilderness."

"And the woman fled into the wilderness, where she has a place there prepared by God so that they might nourish her there a thousand two hundred and sixty days." (Rev. 12:6)

"And when the dragon saw that he was cast to the earth, he persecuted the woman who brought forth the man-child. And to the woman there were given the two wings of the great eagle that she might fly into the wilderness into her place, where she is nourished for a time and times and half a time from the face of the serpent. And the serpent cast water as a river out of his mouth after the woman that he might cause her to be carried away by its current. And the earth helped the woman, and the earth opened its mouth and swallowed the river which the dragon cast out of his mouth. And the dragon became angry with the woman and went away to make war with the rest of her seed, who keep the commandments of God and have the testimony of Jesus. And he stood on the sand of the sea." (Rev. 12:13-18)

"If you love Me, you will obey Me. If you obey Me and keep in step with Me, you can be part of My Bride. For you need to be filled with oil, which is My Word, to be caught up by Me. Yet, should you stay behind I will nourish you, but you will be persecuted by the anti-Christ.

Listen, My people, you are living at the end. You've heard about the end-time many times. If you come to Me and ask Me the truth about the end-time, about the revelation of the time you are living in, then I will open your eyes and give you the wisdom and revelation of Me. Don't be naive, for My Word is truth and every word that proceeds out of the mouth of God will come true."

THE MAN-CHILD TO BE RAPTURED

To be part of My Bride – the man-child caught up to Me in the middle of the tribulation – you need to be filled with oil. This oil is from speaking the Word, reading the Word, therefore, receiving the Sword in your mouth. For you will be transformed if you eat My words and drink My life-giving Spirit. You also need to spend time with Me and wait on Me in silence so that I can fill you with oil from the Father. We will bless you and show you many revelations if you make time for Us and realise that these times before the end is crucial for you to get the oil and the Sword. Anything else you spend more time on than Me, is an idol. For I am a jealous God. I will crush those idols in your life. That will be grace and mercy when I do that!

My child, if you desire to be part of My Bride, come to Me so that I can cleanse you. Ask Me to prepare you for the rapture. I will prepare you, if you ask. Be willing to learn from Me. Be teachable. Lay down all your teachings and doctrines. Come get new wine from Me. Then obey as I lead and teach you for I am your Teacher! Come ask Me the truth. I will not lie to you. I will show you the absolute truth. Just ask the truth from Me and I will show you My truth!

Time is running out, call out to Me and inquire from Me. Come sit at My feet and learn from Me!"

Chapter 8

THE WEDDING FEAST IS READY

8 July 2011

"Yes, the honeymoon will be a 1 000 years. That special day, the wedding day of the Bridegroom (Christ) and the Bride will be the beginning of a marital agreement that will last forever. We will become one, yet divinely two, of one being the Triune God and the other you! We will function as a corporate one. Just like a man and women in a loving relationship. The Bridegroom will love His Bride and His Bride will respect Him. The Father prepared a honeymoon gift for the Bride and Bridegroom of which the secret of this gift will remain locked till the wedding feast. It is the Father's gift!"

I WOULD LOVE TO MARRY YOU, MY BRIDE!

"My Bride will love Me, like a wife loves her husband. She will adore Me as I adore her. Do you love Me like this, My child? Do you love Me this intimately that you will spend forever with Me? You will be called the wife of the Lamb. Do you want to be My wife? What a privilege for Me if you will take My hand in marriage. Will you marry Me? I would love to marry you, My Bride! The date is set, the dress is ready, and the Father is ready! I, the Bridegroom am ready! Did you receive an invitation to this day? Do you want to receive an invitation to this wedding? Do you want to be My Bride?"

"And Jesus answered and spoke again in parables to them, saying, the kingdom of the heavens has become like a king who prepared a wedding feast for his son. And he sent his slaves to call those who had been called to the wedding feast, yet they would not come. Again, he sent other

slaves, saying, tell those who have been called, Behold, I have prepared my dinner: my oxen and my fatted cattle have been slain, and all things are ready. Come to the wedding feast. But they disregarded it and went off, one to his own field and another to his business, and the rest took hold of his slaves, treated them shamefully, and killed them. And the king became angry, and he sent his troops and destroyed those murderers and burned their city.

Then he said to his slaves, the wedding feast is ready, but those who have been called were not worthy. Go therefore to the crossroads, and as many as you find, call to the wedding feast. And those slaves went out into the streets and gathered all whom they found, both evil and good, and the wedding feast was filled with those reclining at table. But when the king came in to look at those reclining at table, he saw there a man who was not clothed with a wedding garment, and he said to him, Friend, how did you come in here without a wedding garment? And he was speechless. Then the king said to the servants, Bind his feet and hands, and cast him out into the outer darkness. In that place there will be the weeping and the gnashing of teeth. For many are called but few are chosen." (Matt. 22:1-14)

"The wedding feast is ready! Do you want to be worthy to be called to be invited to this wedding? If you love Me, you will obey Me. If you obey Me, you will let Me lead you on the path of righteousness. Be obedient, for I will speak to you, for you need to overcome the systems that keep you in slavery."

I AM NOT A RELIGION, I AM NOT IN RELIGION

"If you love Me, obey Me and seek Me for the truth. Do as I instruct and you will be part of My Bride. For many are called, but few are chosen. For My Bride will know who they will marry and the Bridegroom will know His Bride likewise. If I do not know you because you did not seek Me intimately, you will not be chosen. My child, if you desire to know Me intimately, just be in relationship with Me. I am not **a** religion. I am not **in** religion. I AM God, and I know you, yet I desire that you know Me. If you seek Me, I will reveal Myself to you. Daily seek Me, speak to Me, read My Word, for I will manifest Myself to you. Wait on Me in quietness, for your lives are so busy. If you make time for Me, I will reward you if you diligently seek Me. Ask Me for the Father's perfect will in your life and you will find all things work out for good because you love Me. I will bless you and keep you; I will let you feast with Me. I will prepare a table for you in front of your enemies and only goodness and mercy will follow you all the days of your life, because I am your Shepherd.

Come to Me My child, come spend time with Me. I will teach you things you do not yet know. Call on My Name, for the Father continually searches the earth to find those living in righteousness. Those in right standing with Me. Eat and drink Me daily. Eat My Word, which is Me and drink of My life-giving Spirit that is poured out on you as you eat My Word."

"I am the bread of life. Your fathers ate the manna in the wilderness, and they died. This is the bread which comes down out of heaven, that anyone may eat of it and not die. I am the living bread which came down out of heaven; if anyone eats of this bread, he shall live forever; and the bread which I will give is My flesh, given for the life of the

world. The Jews then contended with one another, saying, How can this man give us His flesh to eat? Jesus therefore said to them, Truly, truly, I say to you, Unless you eat the flesh of the Son of Man and drink His blood, you do not have life within yourselves. He who eats My flesh and drinks My blood has eternal life, and I will raise him up in the last day. For My flesh is true food, and My blood is true drink. He who eats My flesh and drinks My blood abides in Me and I in him. As the living Father has sent Me and I live because of the Father, so he who eats Me, he also shall live because of Me. This is the bread which came down out of heaven, not as the fathers ate and died; he who eats this bread shall live forever." (John 6: 48-58)

"As you daily eat and drink Me, you will become full of the knowledge of who I am and you will walk close to Me, for you will know My heart. This is to be in relationship with Me! Surrender to Me and come in submission to Me, for a slave cannot be greater than his Master. I am your Creator and I already know the end from the beginning. Will you trust Me? I love you and I only desire the best for you. Come to Me My Bride, come and run to Me, for I desire to fill you with My love and make an everlasting covenant with you! Come My Bride, for I await your tender heartedness and your love!"

"And the Spirit and the bride say, Come! And let him who hears say, Come! And let him who is thirsty come; let him who wills take the water of life freely." (Rev. 22:17)

"He who testifies these things says, Yes, I come quickly. Amen. Come, Lord Jesus!" (Rev. 22:20)

Chapter 9

MY COMMANDMENTS

9 July 2011

"It is true My child, My commandments I gave to Moses for the people was not to restrict them, but was for them to understand My heart. Who I am. That I am love. All the commandments I wrote down are for love. For if you love Me, you will love Me only (no other gods), you will not have idols, you will not use My name in vain, you will Sabbath rest in Me, you will honour your parents, you will not kill, you will not commit adultery, you will not steal, you will not testify falsely, you will not covet your neighbour.

It is true that the Bible is a divine Romance that I am looking for in My people. Just as I was engaged to Israel, so I am wooing My Bride. I desire a love relationship from you, My child. That is My divine economy (God's plan), that you will enter into a love relationship with Me. For I am your Husband."

"For your Maker is your Husband; Jehovah of hosts is His name. And the Holy One of Israel is your Redeemer; He is called the God of all the earth.

For Jehovah has called you, Like a wife who has been forsaken and is grieved in spirit, even like a wife of one's youth when she has been rejected, says your God."

For a short moment I forsook you, but with great compassion I will gather you. In a flood of wrath I hid My face from you for a moment, but with eternal loving-

kindness I will have mercy on you, says Jehovah your Redeemer.

For this is like the waters of Noah to Me, when I swore that the waters of Noah would not overflow the earth ever again; So I have sworn that I will not be angry with you, nor will I rebuke you. For the mountains may depart, and the hills may shake, but My loving-kindness will not depart from you, and My covenant of peace will not shake, says Jehovah who has compassion on you". (Isa. 54:5-10)

"My desire is for you to love Me. Only Me. If you love something or someone more than Me, that is an idol. I am a jealous God. If I am not first in your life, you will miss it when I speak to you, for your focus is not on Me. You will see the reward of this, focusing on Me and My will, when you turn to Me."

MANY WILL BE DECEIVED

"You are moving into a time where many will be deceived. Things seem to be great and that I am also involved, but that is not always true. For the prince of the world can also do signs and wonders and miracles. Watch therefore that you do not be deceived. For only I will tell you the truth from the lie. Only I can give you sharpness in discernment. This is why it is so important that you remove the idols and make me first in your life, because you will be deceived if I am not.

Seducing and deceiving spirits has entered into churches and ministries. When I am first in your life and you asked Me for truth, I will open your eyes for truth and you will see. Many of My people follow blindly after other people, pastors, ministers and leaders. Come and ask Me if someone speaks the truth. Not all teaching was birthed from My Holy Spirit. Many teachings were birthed by seducing and deceiving spirits. Test the teaching with Me. Many teachings cannot be tested against My Word for many things were not written down, but I will show you if something is true or false.

My people, it is urgent, urgent times. If you walk in My light and you abide in My presence, I will teach you the truth concerning all things. Follow Me, for I am the true vine."

"I am the true vine, and My Father is the husbandman.

Every branch in Me that does not bear fruit, He takes it away; and every branch that bears fruit, He prunes it that it may bear more fruit. You are already clean because of the word which I have spoken to you.

Abide in Me and I in you.

As the branch cannot bear fruit of itself unless it abides in the vine, so neither can you unless you abide in Me. I am the vine; you are the branches. He who abides in Me and I in him, he bears much fruit; for apart from Me you can do nothing. If one does not abide in Me, he is cast out as a branch and is dried up; and they gather them and cast them into the fire, and they are burned.

If you abide in Me and My words abide in you, ask whatever you will, and it shall be done for you. In this is My Father glorified, that you bear much fruit and so you will become My disciples. As the Father has loved Me, I also have loved you; abide in My love." (John 15:1-9)

I AM CALLING FOR UNITY IN MY CHURCH

"When you don't follow Me, but follow after a person, pastor or leader, you will be deceived and you will walk in darkness. My Body should walk together. Not sheep leading sheep. Only I, the true Shepherd, can lead the sheep. My Body can learn from each other, build each other and mingle together, for if there is unity in My Body, Satan trembles.

I am the Head, the only head of the Church. Every member of My Body should listen to Me first and foremost before listening to any other person, pastor or leader. When I lead you, you will be on the path of righteousness and you will be under My protection and I will teach you the truth. Your eyes will be opened and you will be serviceable in My hand.

Do you want to be My disciple or another's disciple? Only if you are My disciple, you will be taught the truth and you will have divine protection. No person, pastor, leader, church or ministry can be your covering. Is a human or system your covering? How safe is that? I, the Lord God, am the only true covering, for I will hide you under the shadow of the Almighty. What human can give you this covering?

Therefore, in My Body (church) all are equal. None is above the other. My Body must function on the ground of unity. Remove the division from among yourself. If you make me the Head of the church and focus on Me only, the divisions will disappear and My church will become My Body. Open your eyes, open your ears, for I am going to shake, uproot, pluck, pull, destroy, and break down My church. For I want her to become My Body. I will then plant and build her and she will give abundant fruit.

I am calling for unity My church. Oneness! For if you remove the divisions, the man-made doctrines from within your walls, you will start to function in unity. The Father's eternal plan is that you function in unity. All We see is division! Don't you see it? Are you so blinded by religion and tradition that you cannot see that everyone is doing his own thing based on man-made doctrines? Religion and tradition kills the work of My Spirit. My Spirit will not enter where man-made doctrine operates. I am not in your religion and traditions! I hate it!"

"**Hypocrites! Well has Isaiah prophesied concerning you, saying, this people honours Me with their lips, but their heart stays far away from Me; But in vain do they worship Me, teaching as teachings the commandments of men." (Matt. 15:7-9)**

"Remove your man-made laws, your traditions, and your religious notion out of My Father's house! I am looking for people who stand on the ground of unity, where only I, Christ am the Head and centre. That church is the church of Philadelphia. All other churches can learn from them."

"And to the messenger of the church in Philadelphia write:

These things says the Holy One, the true One, the One who has the key of David, the One who opens and no one will shut, and shuts and no one opens: I know your works; behold, I have put before you an opened door which no one can shut, because you have a little power and have kept My word and have not denied My name.

Behold, I will make those of the synagogue of Satan, those who call themselves Jews and are not, but lie -- behold, I

will cause them to come and fall prostrate before your feet and to know that I have loved you. Because you have kept the word of My endurance, I also will keep you out of the hour of trial, which is about to come on the whole inhabited earth, to try them who dwell on the earth.

I come quickly; hold fast what you have that no one take your crown." (Rev. 3:7-11)

"The Father desires unity in My Body. I am calling forth unity in My Body. Remove the division and focus on Me. Only in unity My Body will be able to stand the darkness that is about to come over the world. Be serious about Me."

"He who overcomes, him I will make a pillar in the temple of My God, and he shall by no means go out anymore, and I will write upon him the name of My God and the name of the city of My God, the New Jerusalem, which descends out of heaven from My God, and My new name. He who has an ear, let him hear what the Spirit says to the churches." (Rev. 3:12-13)

Chapter 10

MY TORCHBEARERS

10 July 2011

"I am sending out My torchbearers. Those who have received the light from My fire, I am sending out all around the world. They will light many fires with this authority and they will take the Light, which is Me, to many nations. Those torchbearers are My sons. Because I've chosen My sons before the foundation of the world."

"Even as He chose us in Him before the foundation of the world to be holy and without blemish before Him in love, predestinating us unto sonship through Jesus Christ to Himself, according to the good pleasure of His will." (Eph. 1:4-5)

"As darkness comes over the earth, likewise I will increase My light in the torchbearers. Many will be drawn to the Light in those torchbearers for I am the Light within them. My sons are in Me and I am in them. I was the first Son born of many sons chosen by the Father. The Father desires many sons, for we are divinely and corporately mingled to the Father's plan."

"For we are His masterpiece, created in Christ Jesus for good works, which God prepared beforehand in order that we would walk in them." (Eph. 2:10)

"Remember, I am Jehovah your God who will bring you out of the land of Egypt, out of the slave place. Remember, I will take you out on eagle's wings and My intention is to bring you into the Promised Land. Land of milk and honey. That will be the Millennium when I will come to restore My Kingship and My people will help Me restore the earth. It will then be the land of milk and honey.

My people, the wilderness time will happen soon. You're standing at the beginning of this. Therefore, ask Me to lead you out of this house of slavery, this soul-life, this worldly life. For only My work that I speak and bless will remain. All else will be in vain. You do want to be left behind in Egypt and even in the wilderness? Without Me, you will die. Leave your Egyptian mindset and soul-life because you have the choice what to sow. For you will reap your choices in eternity."

BE HUMBLE AND SUBMISSIVE TO ME

"Listen to Me when I speak. Though the things I ask may seem hard or difficult, it will not be so, for I will send My Spirit and My angels to help you, guide you, minister to you and protect you. All these 'difficulties' will be there to test you, to see what is really in your heart. Then you will know and I will know what is in your heart towards Me. Just be humble and submissive to Me. Love Me, obey Me and you will find favour in My eyes and I will bless you. For you will see Pharaoh, you will see the plagues and you will see My divine protection.

I will wondrously guide you in the wilderness with My cloud and fire, feeding you with My manna and water. Will you come out of the luxuries of the soul-life? The world-life you grew so affectionate to? Will you fully obey Me and be in a loving relationship with Me? I desire a people that will worship Me in Spirit and Truth, daily. Not just on a Sunday morning. It should be a daily devotion to Me. Sacrifice your Egyptian lifestyle daily, your soul-life entertainment. Will you sacrifice and lay down your soul-life entertainment for Me?

I am the rock and out of Me flows living water. I will quench your thirst with everlasting living water. Come drink from Me. O My people, I died for you, to be resurrected in order to be poured out into you. To be one with you. I cannot become fully one with you while you wander in Egypt. I want to enlarge Myself in you. Come aside, for I want to set you apart. You will not be off this world, but only in this world. Come My child, come to Me, desire Me, seek Me, call on Me. For I long to manifest Myself as the Triune God to you."

THE ULTIMATE TEST

"This is now the time for the ultimate test on the human race. You are now at the beginning of the end. The Exodus out of Egypt, into the wilderness will start now. This will be a test of your love for Me, your endurance and your obedience toward Me. No more playing with religion, for I am not in it. I desire a real relationship with you.

Many things are about to happen. You are blinded if you do not see that we are at the beginning of the end. Ask Me to remove the veils from your eyes, for only absolute obedience to Me will see you to the end. If you cannot discern My will, ask Me why you cannot discern. Set time apart for Me, for the time is running through the hour glass, for behold I come quickly!"

MY FRIENDS WILL BE WATCHING

"For no man knows the day or the hour of My coming. But for those who abide in Me, love Me, obey Me, honours Me, I will reveal the season of My coming. For I will come like a thief in the night, but I am not a thief to those I call friend. My friends will be watching, for they will discern their Lord is coming, in the season I will make known to them."

PRAYER

Creator God and Eternal Father I acknowledge You as my Lord!

Jesus Christ, my Redeemer, I praise and worship You. I believe You died on the cross of Calvary for my sin. I believe You rose from the dead and are seated at the right hand of the Father. You redeemed me with Your blood and I am Yours. I want to live for You alone and I want to be ready when You come again to take me to You.

I stand guilty before You, Father and others for my sinful way of living and my faulty actions. I confess my sins and shortcomings. As Your child I now come to You with a contrite heart asking for forgiveness. Wash me in the blood of the Lamb, and I shall be whiter than snow and no sin shall longer count against me. I thank You.

I forgive every person that has ever wronged me in any way.

Protect me against the evil one.

Holy Spirit, show me any hindrances in my life that will stand in the way of fulfilling the Father's will in my life.

Arouse in me a willing spirit and equip me, o Lord, with obedience at all times to obey the call of Your voice. Use me in Your Kingdom and grant me Your grace. AMEN.

Repeated from the Introduction: The Lord said the following to me ... The book would be for the remnant, for His Bride. The book would be about the preparation for the King's return and for those who did not know, to be warned. "This will be a gift for My Bride. It is for those who love Me, for those who are seeking the truth, who called out 'Lord, tell us more, only the truth Lord'. The book will be about Jesus. Jesus is the key, Jesus must be your focus and Jesus is your destiny."

Prepare For Jesus' Return By Reading

All The Books By Deborah Melissa Möller

The Final Call

The Exodus

My Son David

True Maturity

Available as paperbacks and e-books through

Amazon.com

Smashwords.com

bn.com (Barnes and Noble Bookstore)

Made in the USA
San Bernardino, CA
18 September 2015